Genre Historic

MW00476192

Essential Question
How do inventions and technology affect your life?

A Better Way

by Sandy McKay
illustrated by Seitu Hayden

CHAPTER 1 Washing Day

It was a beautiful summer day, and Wendy Wilson was drawing in her notebook. She could hear her twin sisters, Margaret and June, playing hopscotch. Her brother, Thomas, was riding his bike, and her father was at work in town.

It was Monday, which meant it was washing day. Wendy's mother sprinkled soap flakes into the large washtub. Then she used the paddle to move the dirty clothes back and forth in the water. Stirring the clothes was hard work, and it took a long time for them to get clean.

Wendy's grandmother, meanwhile, was rinsing clothes as they came out of the washtub and before they were put through the wringer.

"Come and give us a hand, Wendy," her grandmother called when they were ready to feed the rinsed laundry into the wringer. The job required a team effort.

Wendy promptly put down her notebook and went to help her mother and grandmother.

Today there were mountains of sheets and pillowcases that had to go through the wringer. Wendy's mother guided the wet linens through the rollers while Wendy turned the handle that powered them. Her grandmother collected the sheets as they came through the rollers, ready to be hung on the line.

While turning the rollers, Wendy was thinking, "Why does washing have to take up so much time?" When Wendy grew up, she did not want to spend her life doing laundry.

After she had helped with the sheets, Wendy took out her notebook and began sketching. She liked to understand how things worked—she even created her own inventions. It was a challenge thinking up new ideas, and she loved tinkering with machines. She made things out of old parts and pieces of timber or metal that were lying around in the toolshed. Once, she even invented a bicycle-powered milkshake maker!

For her eleventh birthday, Wendy's father had given her two notebooks and a brand-new pencil with an eraser. It was exactly what she had wanted, and she had already filled half a notebook with ideas for new inventions.

Wendy's mother wiped her brow and sighed deeply. "Mother always looks exhausted on washing day," she thought.

Her mother picked up the basket of laundry and began hanging the clothes on the clothesline. Any garments that did not fit on the line would be dried inside by the fire.

"There must be a better way to complete this monumental task," Wendy complained.

Her grandmother laughed. "You should have seen how we did the washing when I was a girl," she said.

"What was washing like in the old days?" asked Wendy.

Her grandmother grinned broadly. Wendy was always teasing her about "the old days."

"Decades ago, we had to cart water from the well, then we boiled it in a huge copper pot," replied Wendy's grandmother. "Washing technology was very primitive back then."

"When I grow up, I'm going to be an inventor, and the first thing I'll invent is a better washing machine!" Wendy declared.

Wendy's grandmother hugged her oldest granddaughter. "I'll let you get on with that then."

Wendy thought about her mother's birthday, which was the next day. Tuesday was ironing day, and Wendy knew what she was giving her mother this year. She would have to get up exceptionally early in the morning.

CHAPTER 2 Ironing Day

The next morning, it was still dark when Wendy climbed out of bed, and it felt like the middle of the night when she crept into the kitchen. Today she was going to do all the ironing as a birthday present for her mother. Wendy smiled to herself. She did not think anyone should have to do ironing on her birthday.

The coal-fired stove was still smoldering from the night before. Wendy took the irons from the rack above. She had watched her mother do it many times, but she had never actually ironed anything herself. First she spread the blanket on the table and laid an old sheet on top, then she put the two irons on the stove to heat. Her mother always used two, because that way one was always hot.

But how did you know when it was hot enough? Wendy was not sure. She sat on the chair and shivered.

The pile of ironing her mother had folded the night before looked like a mountain. The clock chimed loudly in the hallway. It was only five o'clock, and Wendy had never been up before dawn before.

Just then a shadow appeared in the doorway.

"What are you doing up so early?" It was Wendy's grandmother, wearing her bathrobe and slippers.

"I'm doing the ironing," answered Wendy, "as a present for Mother's birthday."

"Looks like you could do with some help," said her grandmother, taking an iron from the stove.

Wendy watched her grandmother spit on the iron. As it sizzled, she pointed out, "That's how you tell if it's hot enough."

Wendy's grandmother took the first iron and slid it over a tablecloth. Just like magic, the crinkles flattened out.

"There. Now, you try."

Wendy took the same iron and pushed it gently along the length of the tablecloth.

"The trick is to keep it at the right temperature," her grandmother commented. "And don't leave it in one place too long."

Wendy took her mother's apron from the pile and carefully guided the iron over the fabric. There were still two huge piles of laundry to do. Thank goodness her grandmother had offered to help.

Wendy's grandmother stood beside her, directing the hot iron over the linens. After they'd finished pressing all the dishtowels and tablecloths, they sat down in front of the fire.

"Grandma, what was my mother like when she was my age?" Wendy asked.

"Gosh," she replied. "Your mother loved to dance. She used to dance all over the house, and she wanted to be a dancer when she grew up. I'll show you some photographs."

Wendy's grandmother took the photo album down from the bookcase. Wendy squinted at the tiny black-and-white photographs. Her mother's glossy, dark hair hung in soft, shining ringlets and looked as smooth as silk.

"She was very pretty," said Wendy as she flipped through the photo album.

Wendy's grandmother patted her hand. "We had better get back to work if we want to get all this ironing done."

The ironing took longer than Wendy had thought, but with her grandmother's help, they managed to get the job done by the time her mother was awake.

When Wendy's mother saw the neat and tidy stacks of clothes, she could not stop smiling.

"You really are a considerate girl," she said, hugging her daughter tightly.

CHAPTER 3 Mother Becomes Sick

It was October, and the autumn leaves were falling from the trees. The days were getting shorter, and most of the laundry had to be dried inside on a rack that hung above the fire. The colder weather also brought coughs and colds to the Wilson household.

One day when Wendy arrived home from school, the house was unusually quiet. Her grandmother stood at the door, looking worried. "Your mother's cold has turned into bronchitis," she said. "The doctor says she needs ten days of bed rest."

"Who's going to cook our dinner?" asked Thomas.

"Who's going to do the laundry?" asked Margaret.

"We'll all help out," said their grandmother. "It won't do us any harm."

The next few days were busy. Wendy helped her grandmother with the washing, and Margaret and June did the dishes instead of playing. Thomas chopped firewood, and Wendy's father helped with the ironing.

"I hadn't realized how difficult this is," he said, pushing the iron clumsily over his shirt.

Wendy took her mother hot milk in the mornings and a steaming bowl of vegetable soup after school.

Her mother lay quietly in bed, propped up with pillows. After ten days, the color slowly returned to her cheeks, and she began to breathe normally again.

Between chores, Wendy continued drawing in her notebook, thinking about laundry more than ever. She knew from experience how much time her mother spent getting everything clean. She would love to invent something that could do the job better and faster. She would design a machine that was easy to use.

What they needed was a washing machine with a paddle that moved by itself. Also, if the water could flow in and out of the sink, then the rinsing and washing could all be done in the same washtub.

Wendy scouted around the toolshed for ideas. She tried to make her own miniature machine using an old crank handle she found in the street. The crank handle, which had been used to start a car, was made of metal and shaped like the letter L.

With her father's help, Wendy made a hole in a tin drum and inserted a piece of pipe for drainage. But it was hard to make the hole the right size, and it kept leaking. She also had to figure out how to keep the water moving around by itself!

Wendy sketched and thought hard, but she could not come up with a solution.

CHAPTER 4 A Surprise Arrives

One day, after Wendy's mother was well again, her father arrived home from work with a basket of oranges. The children rushed to greet him.

"Oranges!" shouted the twins. "We love oranges!"

Oranges were a rare treat in the Wilson household.

"What's the occasion?" asked Wendy's mother, putting down her laundry basket.

"I received a promotion at work," said Wendy's father, looking pleased. Then he gave Wendy's mother a hug.

"Maybe with a little more money coming in each week, we can finally afford to buy something that will make your life easier."

Wendy's mother looked puzzled, and Wendy was confused, too. What could they buy to make her mother's life easier?

Two weeks later, Wendy's father announced that he had another surprise.

Just then, a delivery truck pulled up. They watched as two men struggled up the path with an enormous box.

"Stay inside," said Wendy's father, going outside to meet them. "No peeking!"

After what seemed like a long time, he called everyone onto the side porch. There before them stood a brand-new washing machine!

"Don't forget to plug it into the outlet," said the deliveryman.

"Plug it into the outlet? It is electric?" Wendy lifted the lid and looked inside the machine. It was so new that it gleamed. She squirmed with excitement. The machine actually looked like some of her drawings!

The next Monday, Wendy's mother tried out the new machine. She filled the machine with water, put the washing in, and sprinkled the soap flakes on top. When she turned it on, the machine shuddered into action. The paddle-like agitator was powered by electricity, which meant no one had to stir with the paddle.

The best part was the wringer. The wringer was a smaller version of the one in the yard, and it was attached to the machine. Even better, it could be swung over the sink.

After the clothes were washed, Wendy's mother fed them through the wringer and watched them drop into clean water. Once the clothes were rinsed, she put them through the wringer again before placing them into a basket.

"Oh, the wonders of modern engineering!" Wendy's mother exclaimed.

In no time at all, the washing was ready to be hung on the line.

Wendy watched, sketching a picture of their new washing machine in her notebook. She labeled its different parts, her brain buzzing with ideas for improvement.

"It's a lot better than the old technology, isn't it?" said her grandmother, looking over her shoulder.

"Grandma, you know how you grew up in the old days?" asked Wendy.

"Yes …" her grandmother smiled, waiting for the next question.

"You didn't know they were the old days, did you?"

"No, because they weren't the old days then. They're only the old days now."

"So one day when *my* children grow up, *these* will be the old days, won't they?"

"That's right," replied her grandmother.

"So that means that this washing machine will be old. And there will be something new in its place."

"Probably."

Wendy thought carefully before she said, "I think that one day, someone will invent a washing machine that runs all by itself. And it will be able to wash *and* dry the clothes at the same time."

"Do you?" asked her grandmother, astonished. "Do you really?"

Wendy nodded.

"That sounds like a magical machine to me!" said her grandmother.

Respond to Reading

Summarize

Use important details from *A Better Way* to summarize the story. Your graphic organizer may help.

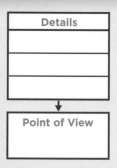

Details

↓

Point of View

Text Evidence

1. What features of *A Better Way* indicate that the story is historical fiction? **GENRE**

2. Describe the point of view from which this story is told. Give examples from the text. **POINT OF VIEW**

3. Find a synonym for *glossy* on page 8. **SYNONYMS**

4. Write about how this story would be different if it were told by Wendy as a first-person narrator. **WRITE ABOUT READING**

A History of Washing Technology

These days, doing the laundry is easy. We have washing machines and driers that do all the work!

Doing laundry was very different in Wendy Wilson's time, when washing was a huge task that took all day.

Washing by Hand

Traditionally, most laundry was washed by hand. Hundreds of years ago, the Romans created large halls called fulleries, which were similar to modern laundromats. Clothes were soaked in sinks. Clay was used to help remove the grease from the clothing. Then workers jumped on the fabric to force the dirt out.

In Wendy's grandmother's time, people used a washboard and scrubbing brush to beat or scrub the dirt out of the fabric.

The McGraw-Hill Companies, Inc. / Jacques Cornell photographer

17

Scrubbing Up with Soap!

The way people washed clothes changed when soap became available. Soap was a new way to break down grease and dirt. In the 1600s, settlers in the United States made soap from ashes and animal fat. The soap cleaned clothes well, but it did not smell good.

In the 1800s, the soap industry began in the United States. Soap was made from animal fats or vegetable oils. It was expensive, however, and it was not until the nineteenth century that ordinary people could afford to buy it.

Easing the Load

The invention of washing machines in the twentieth century made it easier to do laundry. The first washing machines used paddles to move the washing around (similar to the one used by Wendy's mother).

In 1908, the first washing machine powered by electricity was invented by Alva Fisher. Electric machines became common during the 1930s when electricity became more widely available. In 1937, the first automatic washing machine, resembling the kind we use today, was introduced.

These days, washing machines work with the push of a button. New machines use less water and electricity, too. All these improvements make light work of washing.

Make Connections

How important was the use of electricity to the changes in laundry technology? ESSENTIAL QUESTION

In the history of laundry technology, where would you place the system that Wendy's mother used before her dad bought the new machine? TEXT TO TEXT

Focus on Genre

Historical Fiction Historical fiction tells a story that is set in the past. It often gives information about a real event or is based on real facts. Historical fiction gives the reader an understanding of life in the past.

Read and Find A story that is set in the past usually includes dates, events, and clothing or other objects that help show the reader when the story is set. Find details from the story that tell you *A Better Way* is set in the past.

Your Turn

Think of another event involving Wendy and her family—for example, the arrival of their first refrigerator.

Draw a "photograph" for the family album. Use details from the story to help you, and think about the point of view you will show. For an extended caption for the photograph, write a paragraph that describes how the event changes the family's everyday life.